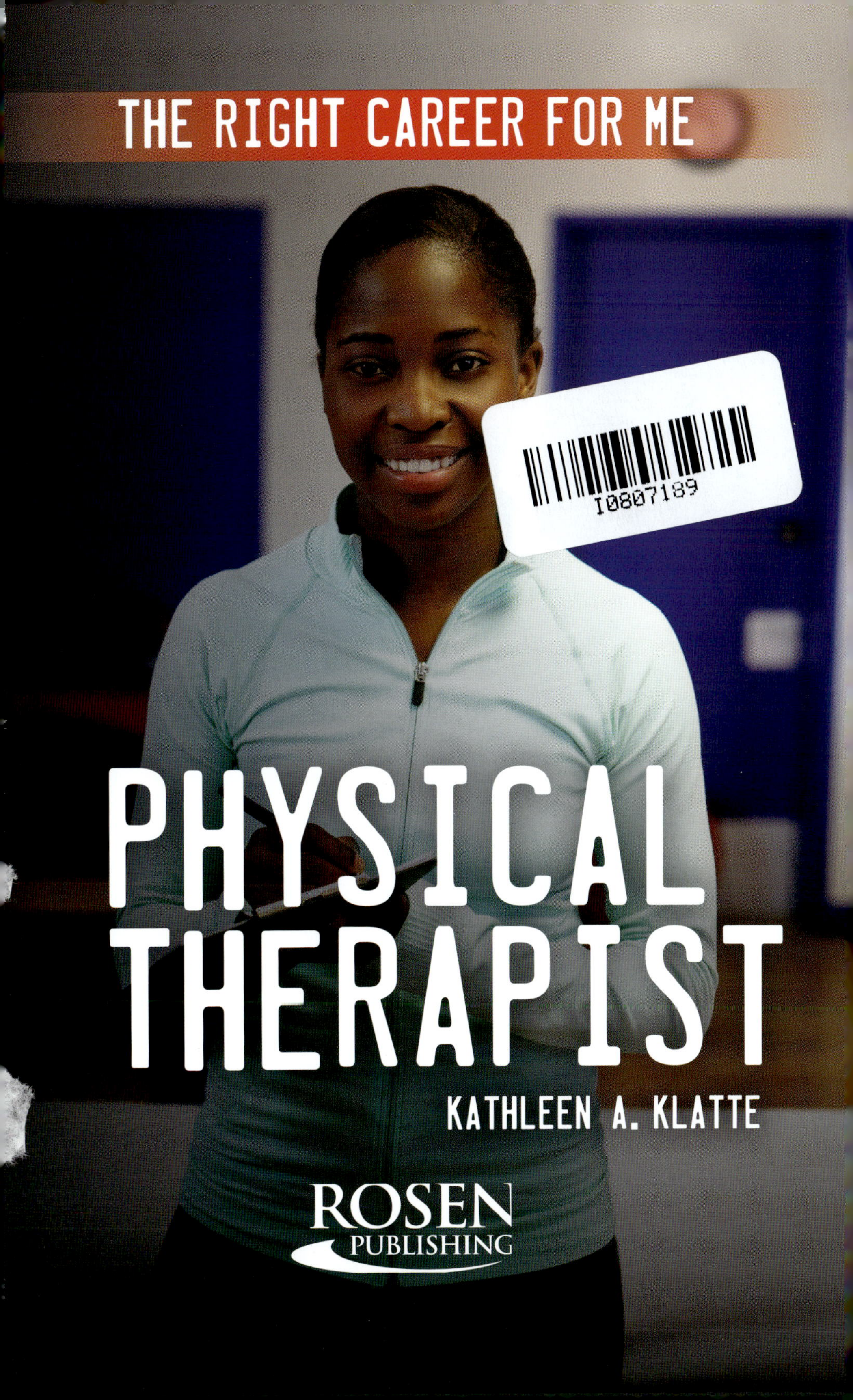

THE RIGHT CARER FOR ME

PHYSICAL THERAPIST

KATHLEEN A. KLATTE

ROSEN PUBLISHING

Published in 2024 by The Rosen Publishing Group, Inc.
2544 Clinton Street, Buffalo, NY 14224

Portions of this work were originally authored by Teppo Harasymiw and published as *A Career as a Physical Therapist*. All new material in this edition was authored by Kathleen A. Klatte.

Cover Designer: Michael Flynn
Intertior Designer: Rachel Rising
Editor: Kathleen A. Klatte

Names: Klatte, Kathleen A.
Title: Physical therapist / Kathleen A. Klatte.
Description: New York : Rosen Publishing, 2024. | Series:
The right career for me | Includes glossary and index.
Identifiers: ISBN 9781499475845 (pbk.) | ISBN 9781499475852
(library bound) | ISBN 9781499475869 (ebook)
Subjects: LCSH: Physical therapy--Vocational guidance--Juvenile literature. | Physical therapists--Juvenile literature.
Classification: LCC RM705.K53 2024 | DDC 615.8'2023--dc23

Manufactured in the United States of America

CPSIA Compliance Information: Batch #CWRYA24. For further information, contact
Rosen Publishing at 1-800-237-9932.

CONTENTS

INTRODUCTION

No matter how tough times are, people will always need medical care, so medicine is usually a solid career choice. But medicine covers many different fields and specialties. Do you like to work closely with people? Are you calm and patient? Do you like to see the results of your hard work? If you said yes, then physical therapy might be a good career choice for you.

When someone has surgery, an accident, or a medical issue such as a stroke, at first, they're cared for by doctors and nurses. Physical therapists, sometimes called physiotherapists (especially outside of the United States) step in to help the patient recover. How soon a patient begins physical therapy (PT) depends on the situation. Doctors need to stabilize some patients before they can begin PT, but someone who's had planned surgery, such as a joint replacement, might start the very next day.

Physical therapists help improve people's ability to move and function in their daily lives. A familiar role of a physical therapist, or PT, is to aid someone who has broken a bone. A doctor repositions the bone and makes sure it can't move until it heals properly. However, after it has healed, the injured limb may have lost its strength and flexibility. A physical therapist can help a patient regain the limb's former abilities.

Helping someone recover from an accident might be the first thing that comes to mind when you think of PT, but it's not the only thing they do.

Physical therapists can also teach others how to make their bones, muscles, joints, and other body parts strong and flexible. They can recommend treatments—generally not involving medication—that will soothe aches and pains after a patient has surgery. They can tell someone when to push his or her body and when to let it rest. They may use tools, machines, or their own bodies to accomplish their tasks. They can help someone learn to live more comfortably with a disease or disorder. These are just some parts of a physical therapist's job.

Physical therapy is a career in demand. PTs are a vital and growing part of the health care workforce. This demand and growth makes physical therapy an essential career. Job stability during tough economic times is one thing to consider when choosing a career. Perhaps just as important is job satisfaction. In many surveys, physical therapists are among the happiest with their careers. Their job involves helping people, and it offers a financial reward as well. PTs can choose from a variety of work environments—hospitals, nursing or rehab facilities, private offices, or even visiting patients in their homes.

Helping an older person stay strong and flexible doesn't just make them feel better, it helps them live safer, more independent lives.

MODERN MEDICINE WITH ANCIENT ROOTS

The concepts that would become modern physical therapy date all the way back to ancient China, when the first cases of movement therapy were recorded. In ancient Greece, there are records from 500 BCE of Herodotus prescribing exercise for his patients, and in 435 BCE, Hippocrates advocated the use of massage and hydrotherapy as health care.

Doctors first began to practice orthopedic medicine in Sweden in the 19th century. The modern practice of PT came into being in the early 20th century. "Reconstruction aides" were trained to help former servicemen recover from horrific injuries they received fighting in the first World War. Doctors also used PT to help polio victims regain full use of their limbs.

Modern advocates of PT look beyond helping patients recover from surgery or accidental injury. They think PT could be a way to preserve joint health, possibly removing the need for surgery and prescription painkillers.

Galen was a physician in 2nd-century Rome. He used gymnastics to rehabilitate injured Roman soldiers.

CHAPTER ONE

WHAT DOES A PHYSICAL THERAPIST DO?

A therapist is a medical professional who helps people with health problems. There are many kinds of therapists who treat many kinds of problems. This includes speech therapists who help people speak clearly, or trauma therapists who help people recover from terrible events.

A physical therapist helps people with issues involving moving part of their body. They assist patients with moving safely and without pain, and help restore body function. Often, a doctor prescribes a patient physical therapy following an accident or surgery. PT helps them recover from the initial trauma and prevent a disability occurring later in life. Some patients are born needing help with their bodies. Others become disabled later in life. All people experience differences in body function as they age.

Physical therapy has been around for thousands of years. As long as people have been promoting exercise for a healthy body or massage to soothe pain, there has been physical therapy. The very earliest records are from ancient China. However, physical therapy as a profession is relatively new.

During and after World War I (1914–1918), nearly every able-bodied young man from every country involved was recruited to fight in the armed forces. Many were killed in action. Many more suffered grievous injuries. Soldiers who had lost limbs weren't able to just return to civilian life—they needed professionals to help them heal and learn how to function with missing or damaged limbs. At first, these people—usually women—were called reconstruction aides. They gave hope to soldiers who had lost limbs or suffered other severe wounds. The aides taught them how to become active again despite their disabilities.

In World War I, soldiers received hasty treatment on the battlefield. Then they might be transported by ambulance or even wagon to the nearest field hospital. It could be weeks before they were brought by ship to a fully equipped hospital.

In 1921, physical therapists formed their first professional association, the American Women's Physical Therapeutic Association. Led by President Mary McMillan, the association included 274 members. By the end of the 1930s, the association changed its name to the American Physiotherapy Association. The group admitted men, and membership grew to just under 1,000. After World War II (1939–1945), physical therapists not only worked with soldiers but also with the many children and adults who were suffering from the disease polio. Physical therapists proved that they were needed just as much as doctors. In 1947, the organization changed its name to the American Physical Therapy Association. It currently represents 100,000 medical professionals.

BOARD-CERTIFIED PT SPECIALTIES

The American Physical Therapy Association (APTA) recognizes 30,000 PTs as board-certified specialists. The first board certification program, focusing on cardiopulmonary (now called cardiovascular and pulmonary) therapy, began in 1981, with the first examination being administered in 1985. As of 2023 there are more than 500 board-certified cardiovascular and pulmonary specialists. The newest board certification available is wound management. The program was approved in 2019 and the first exam was administered in 2022. To date there are 23 board-certified wound management specialists.

In today's health care systems, most doctors don't spend a lot of time with each patient. They assess the problem, then prescribe a treatment, which may include physical therapy. Usually, the doctor will continue to follow up over time to see if the patient has progressed. Unlike doctors, physical therapists work alongside a patient during their rehabilitation. They may see a patient every day or a few times a week. They can see if the treatment is working and, if not, make changes. PTs offer a commitment of progress and time that most doctors aren't able to.

A patient who has had a stroke may have months of recovery. They'll see a PT much more often than a medical doctor.

CHOOSE YOUR SPECIALTY

Physical therapists may practice general medicine, like a family doctor, or they may choose to become board certified in a certain kind of medicine, such as pediatrics. All PTs have some knowledge and experience in all areas of medicine. Physical therapists who choose to specialize are prepared to treat patients within that area of medicine. They study more about certain parts and functions of the body, as well as specific disorders, disabilities, and diseases. PTs who wish to become board certified need to pass an exam in their chosen specialty. Below are the 10 current areas of specialization in physical therapy according to the APTA.

CARDIOVASCULAR AND PULMONARY MEDICINE

Cardiovascular and pulmonary medicine was the first specialty approved by the APTA in 1981. Cardiovascular medicine involves the heart and blood vessels. Pulmonary medicine deals with the lungs. These areas are a combined physical therapy specialization. People who have had heart or lung surgery, or who suffer from diseases of the heart and lungs, may need rehabilitation with a physical therapist who is knowledgeable in these areas. Cardiovascular and pulmonary physical therapists help patients achieve the level of endurance and independence they had prior to surgery and illness.

PEDIATRIC MEDICINE

Pediatrics is the branch of medicine that concerns the care and development of children. The APTA approved pediatrics for board certification in 1981 and administered the first exams in 1986. There are currently more than 2,700 board-certified pediatric PT specialists.

Young patients may have the same problems as adults in all areas of medicine. Yet children need specific treatments since their bodies are still developing. For example, many children don't have the ability or the necessary concentration to lift weights to build strength. The physical therapists assisting them may need to consider other methods of building strength, such as holding a ball. Pediatric PTs work to improve motor skills, balance, and endurance along with other bodily functions. One of the challenges of any sort of pediatric medicine is dealing with patients who might not be able to articulate specifics about their condition as well as parents/caregivers who might be distraught.

Pediatric PTs need a particular combination of gifts. They need to understand the science of small, growing bodies, and the psychology of dealing with kids and their caregivers.

POLIO

Poliomyelitis, more commonly referred to simply as polio, is a contagious virus. Fortunately, it's rarely seen today thanks to the success of the vaccine developed by Dr. Jonas Salk (1914–1995). Before the vaccine was widely used, polio epidemics were common and widespread, affecting thousands of children each year.

Many polio victims displayed general symptoms of illness, such as fever, headache, and nausea. However, polio sometimes attacks the central nervous system, resulting in paralysis. Depending on which muscles and nerves were affected, the patient might have been placed in an iron lung to help them breathe, or they might have had to work with physical therapists to relearn how to walk.

Although most victims of polio were children, one of the most famous American presidents, Franklin D. Roosevelt (1882–1945), was paralyzed by polio as an adult. He walked with a cane and leg braces or used a wheelchair for most of his political career.

Doctors placed polio victims suffering from paralysis in a device called an iron lung to help them breathe.

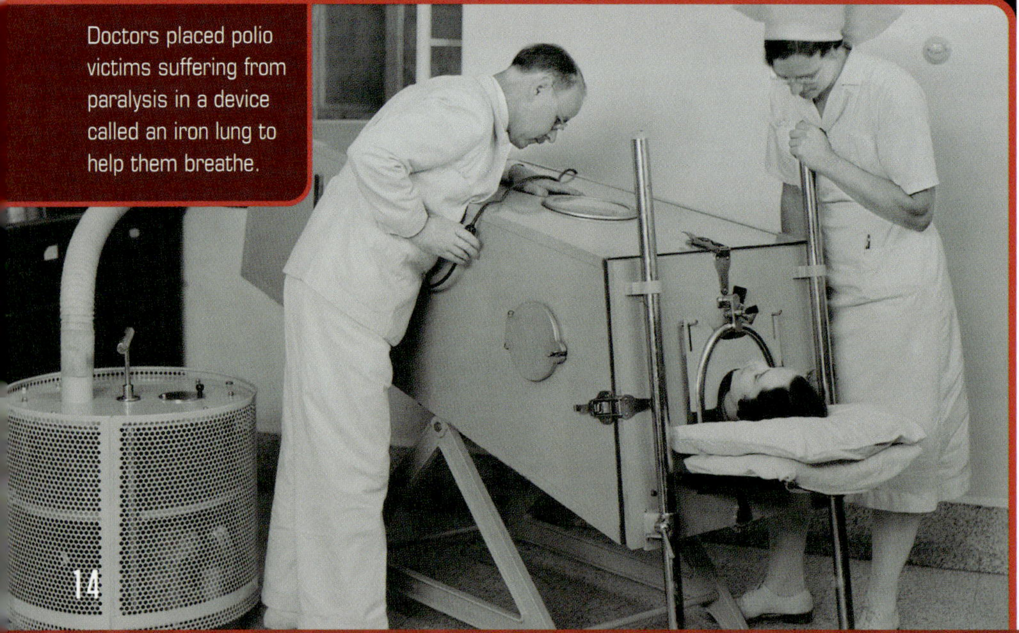

SPORTS MEDICINE

Sports medicine focuses on injuries that happen to athletes on and off the field. The APTA recognized sports medicine as a specialty in 1981 and administered the first exams in 1987. To date there are more than 3,000 board-certified sports medicine PTs.

Sports medicine PTs need to figure out a safe, effective, and speedy way to get an athlete or dancer back on their feet. Part of the challenge of this type of work is educating patients in the reasons not to return to their normal activity level too soon. Athletes and dancers tend to be in very good physical condition and often have professional, educational, or competitive goals they're trying to achieve. They need to work toward prevention of injury and re-injury, as well. Athletic injuries may involve branches of medicine other than the more obvious orthopedic injuries; such injuries may be due to heart or lung problems. Often, a sports medicine PT needs to be a teacher to the athletes and help them understand how to protect their bodies since many injuries are due to repetitive stress. Many professional sports teams employ a physical therapist to work with their athletes. Major dance companies and dance schools also have PTs on staff.

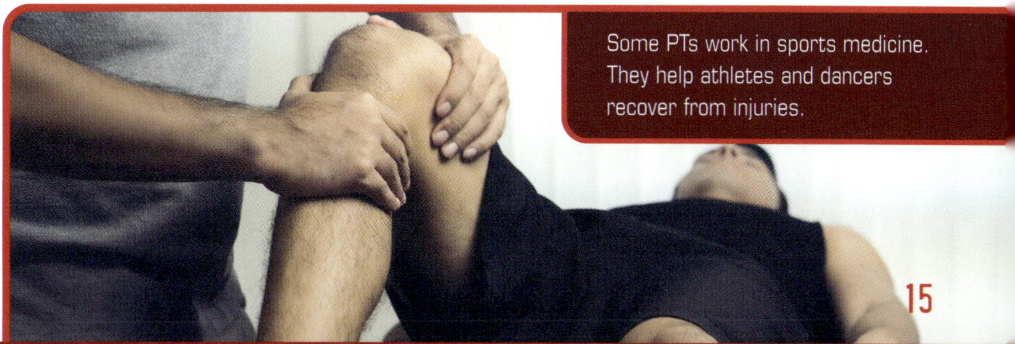

Some PTs work in sports medicine. They help athletes and dancers recover from injuries.

ORTHOPEDIC MEDICINE

Orthopedics is the branch of medicine that deals with bones, joints, ligaments, tendons, and muscles. These are the parts of the body that are necessary for movement. The APTA approved orthopedics as a specialty in 1981 and administered the first exams in 1989. To date there are more than 21,000 board-certified orthopedic PTs. Orthopedics is a basic part of most physical therapy plans. However, as a specialty, "ortho" PTs may help people with back pain, broken bones, hip and joint replacements, and arthritis.

In addition to working with patients themselves, PTs might also be responsible for devising an exercise plan the patient can execute at home. This includes a set of written directions for the patient as well as their family.

ELECTROPHYSIOLOGY

Electrophysiology is the study of the way electricity interacts with cells and tissues in the body. In other kinds of medical careers, electrophysiology focuses on correcting heart disorders, such as an irregular heartbeat. In physical therapy, electrical currents are used to reduce pain. The currents can prevent nerves from sending pain messages to the brain. Electricity can also be used to reduce inflammation, heal wounds, and keep blood flowing through muscles and limbs that a patient is unable to exercise. The APTA approved clinical electrophysiology as a specialty in 1982 and administered the first exams in 1986. To date there are more than 200 board-certified clinical electrophysiologic specialists.

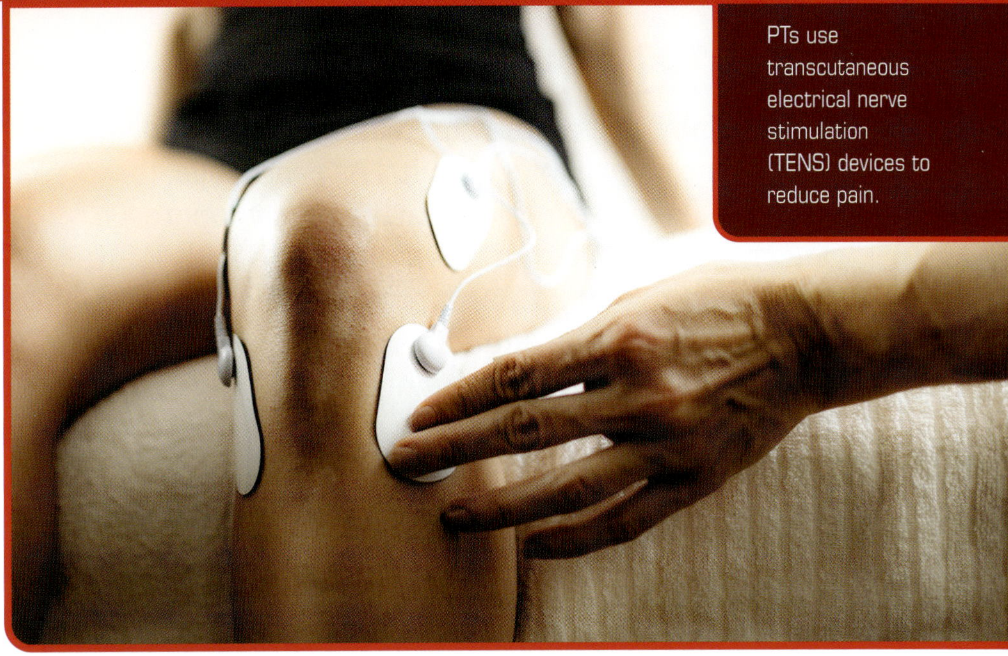

PTs use transcutaneous electrical nerve stimulation (TENS) devices to reduce pain.

NEUROLOGY

Neurology is the branch of medicine that deals with the structure and function of the nervous system. The APTA approved it as a specialty in 1982 and administered the first exams in 1987. To date there are 4,500 board-certified PT specialists in neurology. The brain, spinal cord, and a network of nerves are responsible for sending messages throughout the body to make movement possible. A disease or disorder of the nervous system can result in involuntary movement (such as twitches) or an inability to move (paralysis). Some common neurological problems include stroke, brain injury, Alzheimer's disease, spinal cord injury, and cerebral palsy. PTs work with patients in balancing and walking. Stroke patients require particular care and supervision as they are often on prescription blood thinners, which cause them to bruise very easily.

GERIATRIC MEDICINE

Geriatric physical therapists treat different problem areas in the body in older adults. As people age, they are more likely to experience arthritis, osteoporosis, cancer, Alzheimer's disease, and hip and joint replacement. The APTA approved geriatrics as a specialty in 1989 and administered the first exams in 1992. At this time, there are more than 4,000 board-certified geriatric PTs.

Older patients may need different treatment plans than stronger, more able-bodied people. For example, osteoporosis is a disease that makes bones brittle. Also, some elderly people take prescription blood thinners which cause them to bruise very easily. Patients with these conditions need to be monitored carefully to ensure they don't fall or try to lift more than they're able.

When a patient is prescribed a mobility aid, such as a walker or cane, a PT makes sure it's set correctly for their height and shows them how to use it safely.

Patients with Alzheimer's disease may not be able to tell the physical therapist what is wrong or how a treatment is working. Dementia patients can also have mood swings and be uncooperative about treatments. A geriatric PT must look for other signs to know how the patient is responding to a treatment.

WOMEN'S HEALTH

A physical therapist specializing in women's health focuses on women and their unique needs. Women struggling with pain, disorders, or disabilities may need therapy that is specially designed with their gender in mind. Pregnant women particularly need special care to ensure their growing baby isn't harmed. The APTA approved board certification in women's health in 2006 and administered the first exams in 2009. Currently, there are nearly 800 board-certified women's health PTs.

ONCOLOGY

Oncology is one of the latest fields of board certification for PTs. Oncology is the management of chronic diseases, including cancer and HIV. This includes therapy to help patients recover from surgery and other major treatments and palliative care to maintain mobility and independence. The APTA approved the specialty in 2016 and administered the first exams in 2019. Currently, there are nearly 200 board-certified oncology PTs.

Physical therapy isn't just about crutches and broken bones. Sometimes patients must relearn how to do basic things such as swallowing.

WOUND MANAGEMENT

The most recent physical therapy specialty approved for board certification is wound management. PTs help patients with wounds by devising exercises to help them maintain circulation and retain their range of motion. Proper blood circulation aids in the healing process. Carefully supervised movement helps prevent adhesions—or scar tissue—that builds up between the healing wound and nearby bones or tendons.

HELPING YOUR PATIENT REACH THEIR GOAL

The physical therapist functions as a coach. Just as a sports coach needs to plan a winning strategy, a physical therapist needs to plan an appropriate treatment for their patient. This is one of the many reasons why physical therapists are so valuable.

Because PTs spend so much time with their patients, they get to know them. They learn each patient's strengths and tolerances and what motivates them. For example, a child might be motivated by a small prize, such as a sticker. An older person's goal might be more complex, such as being cleared to return home on their own.

When a patient first meets with a physical therapist, the PT will look at his or her medical history. It's important to know not only the patient's current ailment but also his or her past problems, as well as any medications they might be taking. A PT must be sure not to rehabilitate one area, only to harm another.

Next, they test the patient's strength. The physical therapist assigns a form of therapy that the patient will be able to handle. For example, if a pediatric or geriatric patient needs to build strength in their arm, the PT must know how much the patient can safely lift.

Over time, the PT will learn to "read" their patient. They'll learn when they can cajole them to keep going for a bit longer, and when they really need a break.

It's important for a PT to get to know their patient. For instance, a neurodivergent person might not care for certain textures. It's up to the PT to devise a treatment plan that works for that person.

CHAPTER TWO

TOOLS OF THE TRADE

Physical therapists have all sorts of tools available to help them do their job. Some are simple things, such as rubber balls, resistance bands, and weights. Some are more high-tech, such as whirlpools and TENS devices. Others are things you might not even think of such as modeling clay or "busy boards" marketed for toddlers.

One of the most important tools a PT has can't be bought from a supply shop. It can be taught, to some extent, but mostly, it has to come from within. It's people skills. PTs must be excellent listeners and observers. They deal with patients who might be tired, in pain, or just not feel like doing their exercises. Some patients might not be able to express what they're feeling clearly. A PT must know their patient and be able to read their body language.

One of the things a physical therapist does is measure a patient's endurance. How many repetitions of an exercise can a patient do safely? If a patient has lung disease, they may be able to take only a few steps before running out of breath. In that case, the PT will start the patient with small periods of exercise and then build up to longer periods. Similarly, the PT checks the patient's range of motion—how much they can move body parts. More tests include coordination, balance, posture, breathing, and motor skills.

The PT determines if the patient is capable of living at home, or if he or she would be better off staying at a special facility during treatment. There are benchmarks to aid in this determination. To be discharged from a hospital or rehabilitation facility, a patient needs to be able to walk a certain number of steps, go up and down stairs, and sit and stand steadily, among other things. If the patient is in danger of further injury while living at home, the physical therapist will suggest an alternative setting for treatment.

It's important for the PT, patient, and their family members to all understand the treatment plan.

After looking at all the factors in the patient's life, the PT develops a treatment plan to help the patient's condition and achieve a standard of wellness. The plan may include a series of small goals in addition to the final goal. For example, a patient who wants to go home may need to negotiate six steps to reach their front door. If they live alone, they may need to be able to do things such as reach up to a kitchen cabinet or pour from a carton of milk. These are small goals that can be part of a checklist to help the patient feel a sense of achievement. This is part of a strategy to reach the final goal. A stated goal, purpose, and strategy helps the patient and other health professionals understand why they are doing what they are doing—how the strategies lead to the goal.

Ensuring that a patient has good balance and mobility can help prevent falls.

The treatment plan to achieve the goal or goals may include one strategy or many. It may involve activities performed by a patient alone at home or under the watch of a physical therapist in an office. The treatment may last a few weeks or even years. Everything depends on the condition of the patient. As the treatment plan progresses, it may change. For example, a person with chronic severe arthritis may develop other health issues as they age. The PT needs to take these factors into account when planning any treatment. The physical therapist and the patient will talk about how the treatment is working. The following are some treatments that physical therapists use.

MOTION AND STRENGTH

A PT's job is concerned with preserving or restoring motion and strength. Sometimes this is obvious, such as working with a patient who's recovering from a total knee replacement (TKR) surgery. When appropriate, a PT can plan an exercise routine to help the patient recover. People often think of exercise as active. However, in physical therapy, some exercise is passive; the PT moves the patient's body. Exercise can also be active assisted, meaning the physical therapist and patient work together. In the past, TKR patients used a device called a continuous passive motion (CPM) machine to assist in recovery. These devices aren't used as much anymore, as TKR patients tend to go home the same day as surgery.

Physical therapists teach exercises that help build strength using weights. Other exercises simply use the weight of certain body parts. Strong muscles, joints, tendons, and ligaments also tend to have less aches, stiffness, pains, and injuries. Thoracic expansion exercises (TEE) help make the chest cavity stronger to facilitate breathing. To make the lungs and heart stronger, PTs design programs that work these organs. The heart is a muscle that can be trained like other muscles to regain strength. The lungs and the muscles around them need exercise, too. The exercises that a PT might recommend may involve walking or arm movements to increase the blood flow and breathing rate.

Many illnesses and open-chest surgeries, such as heart surgery, weaken the muscles of the chest. Some people lose their ability to cough, which is important to rid the body of disease. Physical therapists can help build these muscles to help people cough and breathe deeply. This is also essential therapy for people with chronic lung disease, as well as long COVID.

This PT is manipulating the patient's arm. She may not be strong enough to use weights yet.

The full amount of motion that can occur at a joint is called the range of motion (ROM). If the ROM at a joint is less than normal, there may be certain activities that patients can't perform. For example, if a patient's shoulder has a decreased ROM, that patient may not be able to reach an object that is above their head. They may also have trouble getting dressed. To maintain normal ROM, patients must move their joints quite often through their available range. PTs teach patients ROM exercises. It's important to restore ROM if possible, so the patient doesn't damage their other joints by relying too much on one side of their body.

MAINTAINING INDEPENDENT MOBILITY

One of the major goals of physical therapy is to help patients do the things that are part of everyday life. This includes things such as using stairs, being able to get in and out of bed, and using the bathroom safely. PTs understand the muscles and joints that are used for certain movements, like standing up from a chair. PTs work with their patients to strengthen those muscles.

Sometimes PTs must teach people different ways of doing things they've done all their lives, like sitting in a chair. They might advise patients to sit in a straight-backed chair with arm rests, instead of on the sofa. They may break the process down into small steps so that the patient keeps their balance and doesn't put undue stress on their knees or hips.

Many people lose some sense of balance as they get older, which can lead to injuries. Exercises that address balance include stretching, strengthening, and walking. PTs help geriatric patients with balance problems so they don't stop exercising and completing the activities of daily living. They also listen carefully to their patients. If an exercise is causing pain, they try something else.

Gait is the name for all the different parts of walking. Gait training focuses on helping a person develop the easiest and most effective strategies for walking. Treatment involves preventing injuries and developing strategies to increase stability and speed.

Mobility aids are used to help people get to where they want to go. Some mobility aids are walkers, crutches, canes, and wheelchairs. PTs choose the best mobility aid for their patients and teach them how to use it. If the mobility aid is not used properly, it will not be as helpful as it should be and may even be harmful.

They may also advise using different mobility aids for different circumstances. For example, a patient who gets around their house with just a cane might rent a wheelchair to visit a large tourist attraction. Thanks to the Americans with Disabilities Act (ADA), most public places have ramps, doorways wide enough to admit a wheelchair or scooter, and designated accessible parking spaces. This means that once a patient is comfortable using their mobility device, they're not restricted to their home.

If patients lose a part of their body, they may use a prosthesis, or an artificial limb. A device that helps support a weakened muscle or joint is called an orthotic device. A leg brace is an orthotic device. PTs teach patients to move with prosthetic and orthotic devices. Often, balance and coordination exercises are involved in this type of training. They also teach patients how to put on the device correctly, how to remove it, and how to store it when not in use.

Before the ADA, this is what disabled people faced when they went out in public.

ADA accommodations make life easier for other groups of people, such as the elderly—who might have trouble negotiating steps—or parents with small children in strollers.

THE AMERICANS WITH DISABILITIES ACT

The ADA is a federal law that Congress passed in 1990. Prior to that, people with disabilities often had very limited options for going to public places. Basic tasks such as shopping or going to the bank were very difficult because of physical barriers like steps or doorways that were too narrow for wheelchairs.

Thanks to the ADA, most public buildings today have ramps, doors that accommodate a wheelchair, and accessible restrooms. Parking lots have dedicated spaces for individuals with disability license plates or placards for their vehicles. Many stores offer motorized scooter shopping carts.

These accommodations make it possible for people with disabilities to work, go to school, and accomplish many day-to-day tasks independently. It also makes things easier for the elderly and people who are recovering from accidents or surgery.

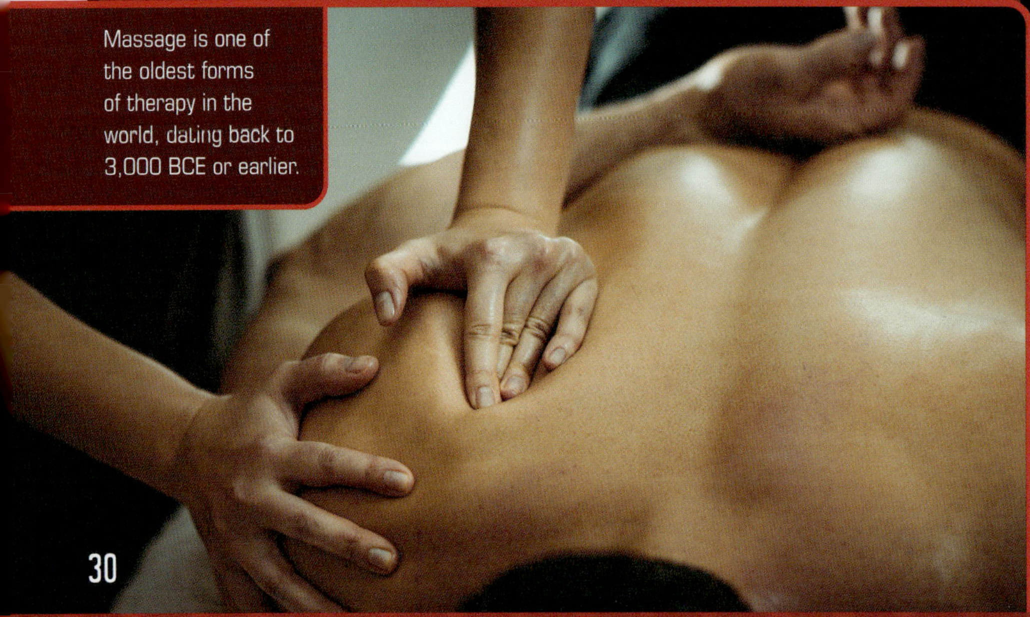

Massage is one of the oldest forms of therapy in the world, dating back to 3,000 BCE or earlier.

HANDS-ON THERAPY

One of the most common types of therapy is called manual therapy. "Manual" means doing something with one's hands. Massage is perhaps the most well-known technique. It can accomplish several goals: pain reduction, muscle relaxation, and increased circulation. Massage is often used in conjunction with other therapies.

Some diseases, such as cystic fibrosis, may involve a buildup of mucus in the lungs. PTs can apply "percussions" and "vibrations" to loosen it. Percussion is force applied to the chest using a cupped hand or device. The patient is placed so that gravity helps to drain the mucus from the smaller air passages of the lungs. The loosened mucus is then easier to cough out. Vibrations or patting the chest help move the mucus as well. People suffering from certain lung diseases might suffocate without these treatments.

Joint mobilization involves a PT moving a patient's joints. The joints may feel tight, stiff, or painful. Loosening the joint can often relieve the pain. To prevent the pain from returning, PTs need to perform other treatments, such as stretching and strengthening exercises. These exercises are tailored to the patient's age, general health, and the medical condition being treated. There are many different movements of mobilization. Some decrease pain, and others help increase range of movement.

HEAT, COLD, AND . . . ELECTRICITY?

Modalities are devices—some simple and some complex—that aid in physical therapy and exercise.

HAIR-RAISING TECHNIQUES

Electricity has been used medically for centuries. The ancient Egyptians, Greeks, and Romans used electric eels to generate electrical shocks for pain relief. By the 18th century, electricity was applied via man-made devices.

- Franklinism generated static electricity by friction.
- Galvanism applied electrical currents directly to the skin.
- Faradism used alternating electrical currents.
- D'Arsonvalization used high-frequency electrical currents.

Doctors and healers used these methods to treat all sorts of medical conditions from gynecology to psychiatry until the beginning of the 20th century. However, in the latter half of the century, modern medicine rediscovered the value of electrotherapy for certain conditions, particularly pain relief.

PTs use electrodes to deliver the electrical current where it's most beneficial. Although the patient may feel a tingling sensation, electrotherapy doesn't hurt.

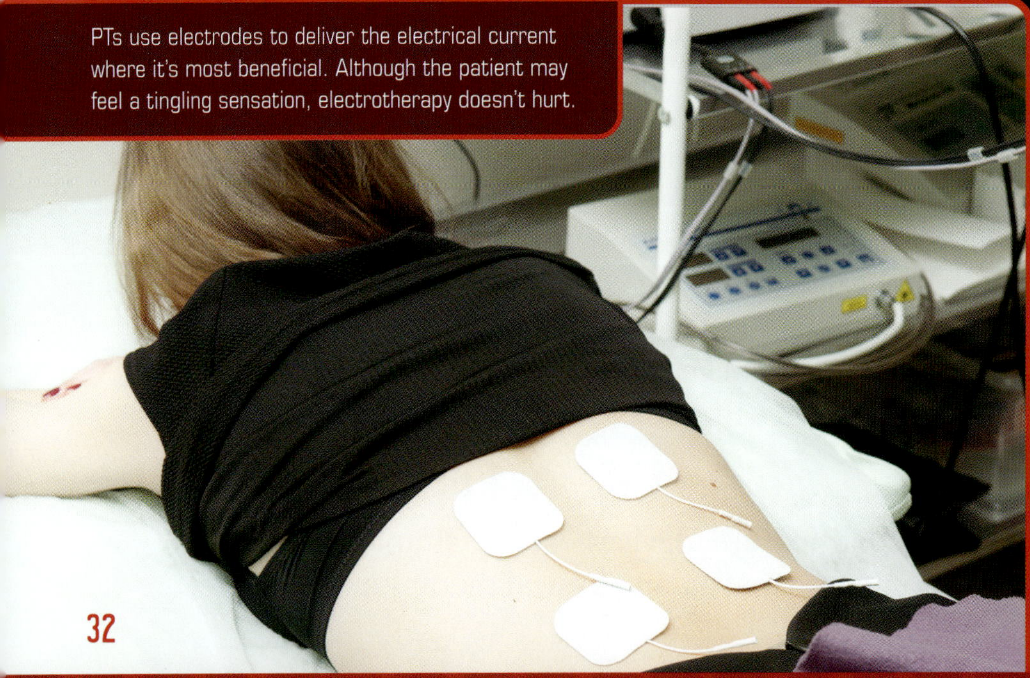

Although the name sounds complex, people use modalities every day for pain relief. You've probably used some yourself.

Heating pads and ice packs are modalities. Physical therapists use heat to relax muscles and improve blood circulation. Some heat packs may be as warm as 160°Fahrenheit (71°Celsius), so a professional is needed in their application. A PT may use heat therapy to loosen muscles and joints before guiding the patient through a series of exercises.

Cold therapy, also called cryotherapy, causes blood vessels to tighten. It can be helpful in reducing swelling. Like many other natural remedies, the use of cryotherapy dates back to ancient Greece. While some athletes use cold water therapy to help strengthen their blood vessels and improve circulation, it's best used under professional supervision, especially if the patient has other health issues.

Ultrasound is another modality. Ultrasound devices create high-frequency sound waves that heat body tissues deep within the body without heating the skin or other tissues close to the surface. The heat increases flexibility and promotes healing. It also reduces pain in soft tissues.

Electrotherapy is the use of electrical currents to relieve muscles and nerves. The heat created brings blood to the tissue, which can speed the healing process. Comatose and paralyzed patients can't move their muscles voluntarily. In these cases, PTs may use electricity to stimulate the patients' muscles to keep the blood flowing and to reduce muscle atrophy. This is called e-stim.

PTs can use electricity to control pain. Transcutaneous electrical nerve stimulation (TENS)

Although massage is usually associated with wellness and relaxation, PTs use specific techniques to help relieve pain and aid healing.

units can be used by patients in a clinical setting or in their homes. If the treatment is to control muscle spasms, the electrical current will help the patient relax. In other treatment plans, the patient may need to tense and then relax their muscles as directed.

Electricity can also be used to conduct medication through the skin. This process is called iontophoresis.

Traction is a pulling force PTs use to lessen pain and increase flexibility. It's been a popular medical treatment since the 13th century. PTs may create traction manually or using a device. Electric traction units create a pulling force through ropes, halters, and straps. This force helps align bones so they can heal properly.

Water is another important part of physical therapy. Treatment using water is called hydrotherapy or aquatherapy. In such therapy, the water supports the body, and heated water decreases muscle stiffness and pain. Hydrotherapy programs, including whirlpools and heated pools, help people with many medical conditions, including arthritis and stroke.

Doctors prescribe hydrotherapy as cardiovascular exercise to improve overall fitness and health. Water "aerobics" classes are popular with older people and those who suffer from arthritis. The water supports their bodies while they exercise without the risk of falling. Participants move their joints and use their muscles without the damage of repeated impacts with the floor, such as would occur during a regular dancercise or step class on dry ground.

Becoming a physical therapist means committing yourself to a lifestyle of personal physical fitness. Your job will involve lifting weights—and sometimes the patients themselves. Massage therapy requires you to have upper body strength. You may need to help patients in and out of wheelchairs or assist them in and out of a pool. Some forms of therapy might include activities such as throwing and catching a ball. And of course, all that equipment needs to be picked up and put away.

To be a PT, you need to be steady on your feet. You need to know how much weight you can safely lift and when to ask for assistance. You need to have good listening skills and the ability to "read" people. All this is in addition to the academic training. Do you think you've got what it takes?

Exercising in a pool eliminates the risk of falling and puts less stress on the skeletal system.

CHAPTER THREE

EDUCATION AND TRAINING

Becoming a physical therapist requires a serious commitment of time and money. In addition to an accredited PT program that usually takes three years to complete, you need a bachelor's degree. If you choose to become a board-certified specialist, that requires more training.

If your high school science classes interest you, you're off to a good start. You'll study the human body in much greater detail before you graduate from a PT program.

Even if you choose not to specialize, you need to understand the many systems of the human body and the ailments that affect them. The educational experience prepares PTs to be truly knowledgeable health care professionals. Excellence in high school science and health classes is a great start. Students of all ages can gain valuable experience volunteering at nursing homes, schools, and day care centers. A variety of volunteer opportunities can introduce future physical therapists to the many aspects of the career

CHOOSING A COLLEGE

Before you start looking into physical therapy programs, you need a bachelor's degree. A few programs combine the undergraduate and graduate degrees. However, physical therapy students should still expect to attend school for at least six years. An undergraduate degree requires classes from different subjects—a well-rounded education. Not only do graduates know about science, but they can also read, write, and calculate. To enter a physical therapy program, the kind of undergraduate degree a student has matters less than the courses he or she took. Undergraduate students should complete courses in anatomy and physiology, biology, chemistry, psychology, statistics, mathematics, and physics.

Completing a bachelor's degree can cost over $100,000, including tuition, textbooks, and room and board. There are ways to lessen that financial burden. State universities are less expensive for residents than private schools. Attending a local college removes the cost of room and board from the equation. You can also complete many basic required courses at a community college, then transfer to a four-year school to complete your degree.

Additionally, more than 75 percent of physical therapy programs require a minimum grade point average (GPA) of 3.0. College students should work with a counselor or adviser to make sure they complete the requirements of the physical therapy program they wish to pursue. Depending on the program you choose, a physical therapy program might cost an additional $100,000.

Before admitting a student, many physical therapy programs require volunteer experience in the physical therapy department of a hospital or clinic. Some schools require up to 150 hours of work related to physical therapy before the student can enter the program. They may also ask for letters of recommendation from teachers or physical therapists. Some schools may require test scores from a graduate exam called the Graduate Record Examination, or GRE, as well.

Start practicing good study habits now. You'll have a lot to learn in college. Aside from needing a good GPA to get into the college of your choice, good grades can help you win scholarships to help defray the cost of your education.

FINDING THE RIGHT PHYSICAL THERAPY PROGRAM

You need to consider many factors when choosing a physical therapy school. The most important factor is the school's accreditation. The physical therapy program must have accreditation by the Commission on Accreditation in Physical Therapy Education (CAPTE). CAPTE is the national organization that reviews each school so that its physical therapy program offers the appropriate courses and a high-quality education. According to the APTA, there are more than 200 accredited physical therapist education programs in the United States.

To help students apply to more than one program at a time, the APTA provides an online application process called the Physical Therapist Centralized Application Service (PTCAS). The PTCAS makes it possible for a single application to be sent to multiple physical therapist education programs. Applications can be quite lengthy and complicated. PTCAS has made the application process much easier. The website includes an extensive list of programs, their requirements, and total cost.

Another major concern is how far away from home the school is located. Room and board are major expenses. Traveling to and from school, transporting all your belongings, and possibly storing them over the summer, can be expensive and time-consuming. Obviously, you want to choose the program where you're most likely to succeed, but these costs do need to be considered.

How much does the program cost? Are you eligible for financial aid or scholarships? How much student debt can you reasonably carry? These are all questions you need to think about when choosing a school.

Other considerations for choosing a physical therapy program include:

- class size
- success of past students in passing the license exam
- success of graduates in getting jobs
- experience and reputation of teachers
- student activities and organizations
- opportunities to practice physical therapy in school
- doctoral and other available professional programs

Be prepared to have some serious discussions with your parents and guidance counselor about your plans. They can help you decide which schools are right for you and how you'll pay for your education.

PROFESSIONAL ORGANIZATIONS

Joining a professional organization is always a good idea. Large professional organizations that operate on a national level often have lobbyists or attorneys on staff who monitor legislation that affects your industry. They provide news about new research and technology, continuing education, and changes to licensing procedures.

Professional organizations often post job listings and have negotiated discounts for certain goods and services available to their members. They also host conferences where members can meet, attend seminars, and view new products.

The most important organization for PTs in the United States is the American Physical Therapy Association. Another is the American Orthopaedic Society for Sports Medicine (AOSSM). Membership in a state or local organization or one devoted to whichever specialty you pursue can also be useful.

You'll probably start looking at schools online. Your guidance counselor is an excellent resource, so don't hesitate to make an appointment and get their advice. Once you have some serious contenders, you'll want to visit the campus and take a tour. Talk to people on campus and see if there's a student or alumni group on social media where you can ask questions. People who've studied at a school can offer valuable and honest information about their experiences.

A clinical residency is a paid job. Residents work under supervision to help them transition from being a student to being a professional.

A degree program in physical therapy usually lasts three years. It starts with basic science courses, such as biology, chemistry, and physics. It then becomes more in-depth about the human body and development, disease, disorders, and therapies. Besides learning in a classroom, students complete internships, called clinicals, in hospitals, clinics, and other settings. Professionals supervise and teach them how to apply their classroom knowledge to real-life situations. When you're looking at schools, ask where your clinicals will take place.

You'll graduate from an accredited PT program with a doctor of physical therapy (DPT) degree. (This is not the same as an MD.) After graduation you can apply for a clinical residency. This is a paid, supervised position in a clinic or other facility.

THE NPTE

After completing your degree in physical therapy, you'll need to pass at least one more test before you can practice. This test is called the National Physical Therapy Exam (NPTE). It exists to ensure that all PTs, regardless of where they trained or where they're practicing, meet the same standards of knowledge and care.

You must take the test on a computer at a testing center. To take the exam, you need to be at least 18 years old, have your PT degree, and be approved by the locality that will be issuing your license. The NPTE is graded on a scale from 200 to 800. A score of 600 is passing. If the test-taker does not pass the NPTE, he or she can take the exam again. There are many resources available to prepare people for the test. The Federation of State Boards of Physical Therapy develops and administers the NPTE. There is a great deal of useful information available on its website, including sample test questions such as these:

A patient has used crutches with a partial weight-bearing toe touch gait for the past three months. When progressed to full weight-bearing, the patient is unable to demonstrate a heel-toe gait sequence with the involved extremity. Which of the following disorders is the MOST likely origin of the gait abnormality?

A. plantar fasciitis
B. fibular (peroneal) nerve palsy
C. heel cord tightness
D. hammertoe

After sitting at a computer station for two to three hours, an individual reports experiencing a sharp, localized pain in the left arm. When asked to show the location of the pain, the individual points to the area of the insertion of the deltoid. The pain disappears when the individual stands up and walks around briefly. Which of the following interventions is MOST likely to correct the problem?

A. isometric strengthening of the deltoid
B. lumbar extension exercises in prone
C. instruction in correct postural alignment in sitting
D. instruction in shoulder active range of motion exercises

Answers: 1. C; 2. C

In high school, you'll use models to study human anatomy, but in medical school, you'll study actual human cadavers.

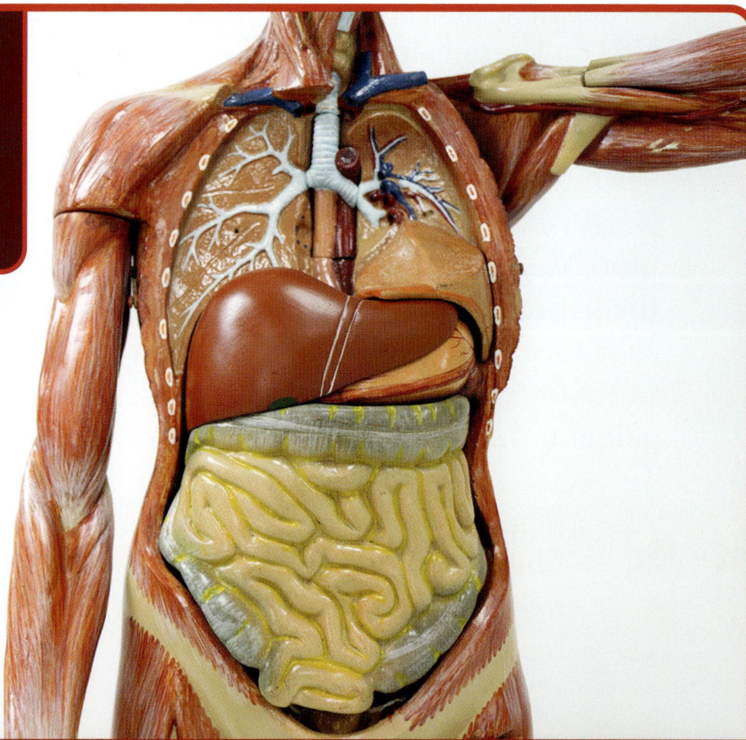

ALPHABET SOUP!

Just what do all those initials after a PT's name stand for?

PT	physical therapist	This is what they're licensed for.
DPT	doctor of physical therapy	This is their degree.

Other initials after these indicate specialties include:

OCS	board-certified clinical specialist in orthopedic physical therapy
SCS	board-certified clinical specialist in sports physical therapy
CCS	board-certified cardiovascular and pulmonary clinical specialist
CEAS	certified ergonomics assessment specialist
CSCS	certified strength and conditioning specialist
CSMT	certified spinal manual therapist
MDT	certified in the McKenzie Method® of Mechanical Diagnosis and Therapy®
MTC	manual therapy certification

So, Jane Smith, PT, DPT, CCS is a licensed physical therapist who holds a doctor of physical therapy degree and is a board-certified cardiovascular and pulmonary specialist.

Are you fluent in a second language? Spanish-speaking medical professionals are always in high demand. So are those trained in American Sign Language (ASL). Or perhaps Italian or Mandarin Chinse are commonly spoken where you live.

WHAT'S NEXT?

The NPTE score is sent to the applicant's state licensing board. This organization is responsible for granting licenses to PTs. Each state licensing board has a set of requirements for the applicant to fulfill. For instance, some states require a criminal background check. The state license helps employers and patients to know that the PT has been tested and found to be competent.

For example, the New York state licensing board requires at least a master's degree in physical therapy from an accredited program and a passing score on the NPTE. Applicants must be 21 years of age. The applicants must submit a fee with a form requesting a license as well. In addition, a license requires that the candidate "be of good moral character." Many states and job sites require a police background check for any criminal activities in a PT's past. There will also be continuing education requirements, to keep a license current.

Some states require additional exams. Students who studied in other countries or whose first language is not English may be required to prove their language skills and knowledge. They can find the procedure to follow through their state licensing board. (In New York state, the Office of Professions is part of the Department of Education. In California, the Physical Therapy Board is part of the Department of Consumer Affairs.)

After receiving a license to practice, physical therapists can enter the working world. Some may wish to specialize in one of the areas described in Chapter 1. To take a specialization exam, the candidate must have a license and more than 2,000 hours of experience working in that specific area of medicine. A test is available for each certification. Upon passing the test, physical therapists are granted a specialization certification. They must retake the test every 10 years. Every three years they must submit evidence of professional practice in their specialty and continuing education.

PTs, like all medical professionals, need to be up to date on the latest developments in their field. They also need to be aware of any new legislation that might affect them.

CONTINUING EDUCATION

Physical therapists are expected to continue learning by participating in classes and workshops. These continuing education courses are measured in continuing education units (CEUs). Each state licensing board requires a physical therapist to earn a certain number of CEUs to keep his or her license.

In California, continuing education is referred to as Continuing Competency. The state requires 30 hours of coursework to renew a PT license. This includes 4 hours of Basic Life Support, 2 hours of Ethics, Laws, and Regulations, and 24 hours of other approved coursework. This requirement keeps PTs educated about the best options and methods of care for their patients, as well as any legal changes that affect their job.

New medical technology is constantly being developed. Equipment and techniques can quickly become outdated, so it's important to stay on top of new developments.

As a PT, you'll spend your entire career learning new information, new techniques, and most importantly, all about new people.

CHAPTER FOUR

BEGINNING YOUR PROFESSIONAL LIFE

As part of their education, PTs participate in clinicals—internships where they work in a variety of professional settings, including hospitals, nursing homes, clinics, and schools. According to the U.S. Bureau of Labor Statistics, about one-third of physical therapists work in the offices of physical, speech, occupational therapists. Another third work in hospitals or clinics. Most of the remaining physical therapists travel to people's homes or work in nursing homes, doctors' offices, schools, and sports and fitness clubs. Wherever they choose, most PTs can expect to work a 40-hour week, which may include evenings and weekends. After graduation and licensure, physical therapists must make the choice: where do they want to work?

WHERE WOULD YOU LIKE TO WORK?

One factor in choosing a first job site is the specialization or area of interest. Perhaps you love kids and work well with them. Or maybe you have an affinity for the elderly. Maybe you're fascinated by electrophysiology or cardiopulmonary therapy. (There are no wrong answers!) There also may be different job titles and responsibilities for physical therapists within each setting. For example, a group of physical therapists within a hospital may have a physical therapy director who oversees their work. In a smaller clinic, a PT may be the sole therapist. Here is a look at places where physical therapists can find work.

HOSPITALS

Physical therapists can encounter a variety of patients in a hospital setting. Some PTs may work only in certain sections of the hospital. Others may work in many. A common patient problem in a hospital is loss of strength from long periods of time in bed. A physical therapist can teach this patient how to regain strength and mobility. They also help patients who are recovering from surgery or accidents learn how to use mobility aids safely.

Burn victims need physical therapy, including active and passive exercise. People with burns suffer pain, itching, and anxiety both from the burn and the healing of wounds. Some studies suggest that massage helps ease these symptoms. Physical therapy can improve movement and function in the burn area and reduce scarring. Doctors treat patients with prescription medication to manage their pain so they can tolerate stretching and exercising.

People in a coma require physical therapy, too. The PT will move and stimulate the patient's

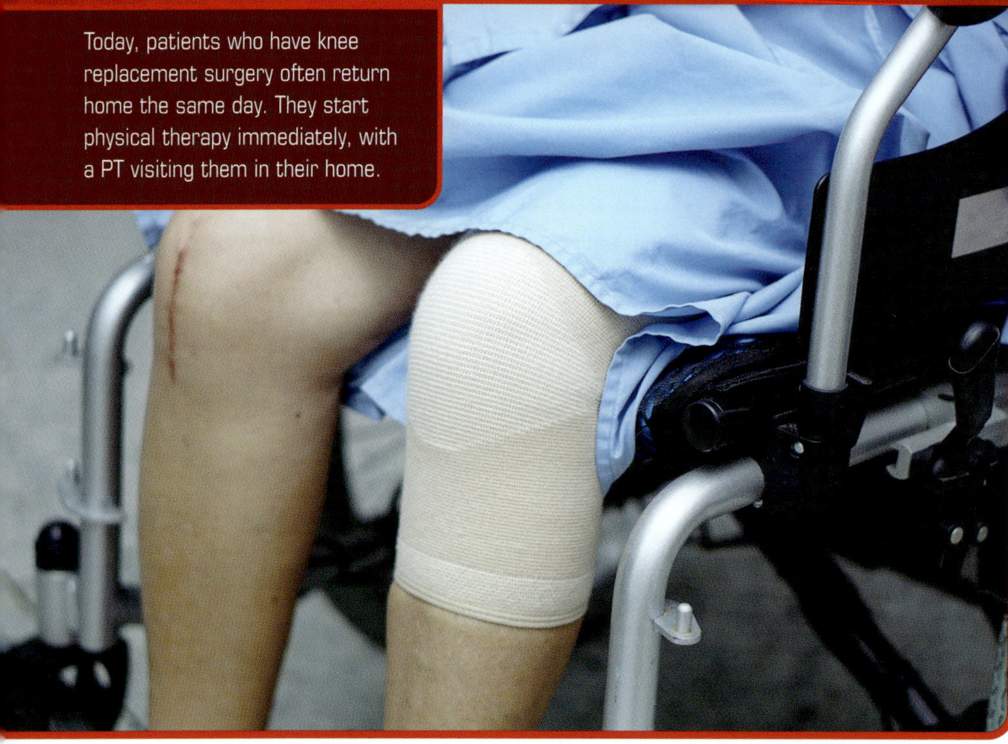

Today, patients who have knee replacement surgery often return home the same day. They start physical therapy immediately, with a PT visiting them in their home.

limbs until the patient can do so independently. Without this treatment, patients' extremities may require amputation.

The duties of PTs in a hospital are as varied as the problems of the patients in the hospital. However, the goal remains getting the patient fit to return home. Studies have shown that the use of physical therapy in hospital intensive care units (ICUs) reduces the amount of time a patient remains there.

REHABILITATION CENTERS

Sometimes patients need a long period of time to recover from an injury or surgery. Doctors may send them to a rehabilitation hospital or center. When a patient needs to stay overnight or longer in a hospital or rehab facility, it's called inpatient treatment. Physical therapists work with these patients until they are able to go home. They'll ask questions about the patient's home: Do you have to climb stairs to enter the home? Is there a bathroom on the same floor as your bedroom? Is there another adult in the home with you? They use these facts to devise a plan to make sure the patient is able to complete day-to-day activities safely.

Patients in rehabilitation centers are often those with severe injuries or conditions, such as spinal cord injuries, strokes, and chronic pain. Some of these people need to learn the simplest of movements. People who lose their limbs through accidents, diabetes, or circulation problems need PTs. They may need to learn to walk with or without the use of orthotics and prosthetics.

Sometimes rehab and residential facilities are in the same building. In these cases, efforts are made to keep different groups of patients separated. PTs in a rehabilitation hospital must work to keep the patient connected to the outside world and optimistic about recovery.

If a patient can't leave their bed, the PT will help them to move their limbs.

CLINICS AND OFFICES

Unlike hospitals and rehabilitation centers, clinics provide treatment for patients who can live at home. Clinics that provide these services are called outpatient clinics. They may be associated with a hospital or be privately owned. They may treat a variety of problems or specialize in one area, such as pain management or sports medicine. Some clinics specialize in physical therapy. Patients seeking help at a physical therapy clinic may be suffering from back, neck, or other limb pain; need after-surgery rehabilitation; or need help caring for wounds. Physical therapists can provide multiple treatment sessions through an outpatient clinic. Doctors' offices often hire PTs to provide treatment as well.

NURSING HOMES AND ASSISTED-LIVING FACILITIES

A nursing home—or skilled nursing facility—is a residential facility for patients who require daily medical care. Some patients must remain in bed, others require assistance with things such as tube feeding. Some require supervision due to conditions such as dementia.

Nursing home PTs practice geriatric medicine. They must keep the elderly patients moving to prevent muscle atrophy. Older patients need to keep exercising to keep their bodies healthy enough for the activities of daily living, such as bathing, eating, and dressing. They may need to learn how to do these things while using a wheelchair or walker. Physical therapists in nursing homes must also aid in easing conditions that afflict the elderly, such as Alzheimer's disease, osteoporosis, and Parkinson's disease.

Another type of residential facility is an assisted-living facility. This type of facility is for people who are more independent but can't live safely on their own. They often feature community activities and field trips for residents.

These facilities aren't only for the elderly. Some younger people who can't live at home unassisted must live in nursing home or assisted-living facilities to receive care.

SCHOOLS

Public schools in the United States are required to provide a suitable education for all students, including those with disabilities. Each student with special needs has an Individualized Education Program (IEP). This is a plan tailored to their specific physical and intellectual needs. A PT in a school might work with teachers, speech therapists, parents, and other professionals to help each child have a school experience that prepares them for life after graduation. Physical therapists in schools may have special knowledge of pediatric medicine to best care for kids.

PT in a school setting might include helping a child with fine motor control.

PRIVATE HOMES

Today, treatments that used to require lengthy hospitals stays, such as knee replacement surgery, are performed outpatient. The patient still requires extensive physical therapy, so the PT visits their home. Sometimes PTs visit patients who can't drive or would have difficulty using paratransit by themselves. In these cases, agencies specializing in home health care send physical therapists to people's homes. It can be a great advantage for patients to have physical therapy at home. For example, the PT can see how far the patient needs to walk from the bedroom to the kitchen. He or she can see how many steps are in the house, and so on.

PT VERSUS PRESCRIPTION MEDICATION FOR PAIN MANAGEMENT

You may have heard the phrase "opioid epidemic" in the news. Opioids are a class of drugs that includes illegal drugs such as heroine and prescription medications such as morphine and codeine. Some of these are derived naturally from the opium poppy and others are created in a lab setting. These drugs are highly addictive if they're not used correctly.

If a person becomes addicted to a drug, and can't obtain it legally, they may turn to illegal sources of medication or even street drugs. This is very bad, because there is no quality control for illegal drugs. People can die of an overdose or from taking contaminated drugs.

So why do doctors use opioids if they're so dangerous? Doctors prescribe strong painkillers such as morphine in specific situations such as surgery, because otherwise the pain would be too great for the patient to bear. Burn victims and patients recovering from joint replacement surgery are prescribed painkillers so they can tolerate the movement necessary for their physical therapy.

Some people suffer from conditions that cause chronic pain. They start out taking over the counter (OTC) medications, but eventually they build up a tolerance to those drugs, so their doctor prescribes something stronger. Prescription pain medications can often have side effects, such as stomach damage, so doctors monitor their use closely.

There are studies, including one from Stanford University, that suggest using physical therapy as an alternative to medication in patients with chronic pain. The study says that patients prescribed PT shortly after their diagnosis are less likely to need prescription pain medication.

CREATING YOUR FIRST RÉSUMÉ

Once you've chosen the type of facility you'd like to work in, you need to start the job hunt. Just as you applied to school, you need to apply for a job position. Are you planning to stay in the same area where you grew up? Near where you went to school? Or have you set your sights on a particular facility?

You should have an idea of the cost of living and commuting when searching for a job. For example, if you live in Westchester County, New

York, there are many hospitals and medical practices to choose from. Westchester Medical Center in Valhalla and Montefiore Medical Center in the Bronx are prestigious facilities with large campuses that offer many specialties. In your job hunt, you need to consider how you'll get to work—via car (gas and parking) or public transportation (a transit pass and possibly limited/inconvenient hours of operation).

The education process gives PTs a lot of experience to present to possible employers. However, physical therapists need to know how to make themselves stand out. A résumé—sometimes called a curriculum vitae or CV—is one of the most important tools you'll use in your job search. It gives the employer a "snapshot" of the physical therapist before meeting him or her. Résumés may look different for different jobs. However, there are some basics that should always be included:

- name, address, and contact information
- college, graduate school, and advanced degrees
- licenses
- detailed lists of professional experience relating to physical therapy
- professional society and organization memberships
- honors and awards
- any other notable skills, such as knowledge of foreign languages or computers

As you progress in your career there will be more things to add:

- continuing education and professional development classes
- teaching activities, including presentations and clinical education
- publications in books, medical magazines, and journals
- research activities

Today, most people conduct their job search online and often apply for jobs online. The APTA website contains a job search portal and offers advice on writing your résumé and cover letter. A cover letter accompanies your résumé and should be tailored to each job you apply for. For example, when applying for a job at a school or pediatric clinic, you might mention that you grew up with younger siblings or worked as a camp counselor, in addition to any pertinent clinical experience or training.

ACING THE INTERVIEW

Once you've submitted your résumé and cover letter, you'll be waiting for a response. Take that time to do some research on the facility you applied to. Think of questions you'd like to ask. Be mindful of how you answer the phone while you're waiting to hear from a potential employer. Keep a pen and paper handy to write down all the details when they call to ask you for an interview.

A job interview can seem intimidating. However, a good interviewer wants to bring out the best in people and an interview shows that the employer is already impressed with the candidate's résumé. Now they want to see how you act in person. The following interview tips can apply to any job opportunity:

- Dress appropriately. Depending on the location and type of practice, you may not need to wear a suit, but at least business casual, neatly pressed. Hair, nails, and makeup should be discreet.
- Arrive early, perhaps 10 to 15 minutes early. Freshen up and take a few deep breaths.
- Bring an extra résumé. Have contact information for any personal or professional references printed out in a neat document.
- Act like a coworker with whom the employer would want to work. Be upbeat. Smile and make eye contact. Be courteous to anyone you encounter in the lobby or parking lot.
- Be confident without bragging. Be honest about accomplishments. State strengths that stand out among other PTs.
- Send a thank-you note after the interview (email is fine). It will remind the interviewer of you, one of possibly many. It shows thoughtfulness and courtesy.

Remember, you'll be shaking hands with your interviewer, and you're applying for a job using your hands. This is not the occasion to show off long, acrylic nails!

OTHER CAREER PATHS

Most people who train for a career as a PT choose to participate in a practice, treating patients. However, there are alternative ways to work within this career. Some physical therapists might find they have a gift for explaining and instructing others. They may choose to teach within a physical therapy program rather than practice. They may instruct in a classroom or supervise students in clinicals. There are special degree programs offered for clinical instructors.

Or they might become medical researchers, studying new and accepted methods of therapy and seeking better ways to improve quality of life for patients. However, some people who are interested in a career in physical therapy may find that they do not have the resources to attend a physical therapy education program. (Two college degrees is a huge investment of time and money!) Or they may only wish to work part time. These people still have career options.

PHYSICAL THERAPIST ASSISTANTS

Physical therapist assistants, or PTAs, work under the direction of a physical therapist. Unlike PTs, PTAs do not examine patients, create a plan of care for them, or decide if they are fully rehabilitated. However, PTAs can guide patients through a treatment plan, collect data on their progress, and report their response to treatment.

Physical therapist assistant programs can be found at universities, community colleges, and technical colleges. PTAs graduate from a two-year accredited program with an associate's degree. PTAs need to pass the NPTE PTA exam. Different states have different rules about whether a physical therapist assistant needs a license or not. The Federation of State Boards of Physical Therapy collects information needed for PTAs in each state. Full-time PTAs can expect to earn about $50,000 per year. About one-third of PTAs work part time. The BLS expects a 24% rate of growth in this field over the next decade.

PHYSICAL THERAPIST AIDES

Physical therapist aides work under PTs and PTAs. They are responsible for keeping treatment areas clean and ready for patient use. A physical therapist aide may also help patients move around in wheelchairs or support them in moving in other ways. Physical therapist aides may also do office work, such as keeping records and filling out insurance forms. They may also answer phones and schedule appointment. Generally, physical therapist aides do not need as much medical knowledge as PTs or PTAs.

Aides are not required to have a degree. They can be hired with a high school diploma and receive on-the-job training. They can expect to earn less than PTAs. People who are interested in gaining valuable experience in physical therapy should consider becoming a physical therapist aide first.

As a PT, PTA, or aide, there are many roles you can play in a patient's recovery.

CHAPTER FIVE

WHY CHOOSE PT?

A day in the life of a PT can run the gamut from exhausting to exhilarating. PTs share in the joy of a patient taking their first independent steps. They also share the frustration of someone who just can't make their body do what they want. A PT can experience all these feelings in a single day. Perhaps it is this variety that draws many physical therapists to their work. Most still believe it is the best profession for them.

A 2021 overview in U.S. News and World Reports ranked physical therapist as No. 3 in Best Health Care Jobs and No. 6 in 100 Best Jobs. That's pretty impressive! Physical therapy is rated below average for stress and average for work-life balance.

In a previous survey, PTs listed some of their favorite things about their job:

- working face-to-face with people
- seeing a patient progress toward wellness
- spending time with patients
- making independent decisions
- encountering a variety of situations
- choosing to work normal work hours in most situations
- wide variety of workplaces, from hospitals to private homes
- positive outlook of the future job market

HOW MUCH MONEY WILL YOU EARN?

According to the U.S. News and World Report overview, PTs can expect to earn between $77,000 and $100,000, with the median wage being about $93,000. Salary depends on many factors. Within an organization, there may be different positions of authority and ranking. Another consideration is the experience of the PT. A physical therapist just hired from graduate school will likely earn less than a PT with 10 years of experience. Another aspect is location. Major cities such as Manhattan, Chicago, or Los Angeles have a higher cost of living and professional wages tend to be higher. The type of facility where you choose to work is another salary factor.

According to the U.S. Bureau of Labor Statistics, there were more than 200,000 physical therapists working in the United States in 2021. The BLS website maintains up-to-date salary information, including how job site and specialization impact earnings.

Seeing a patient achieve their goals is one of the best parts of being a PT.

PHYSICAL THERAPISTS IN THE MILITARY

As previously mentioned, the roots of modern physical therapy began in World War I. It was the largest military mobilization in history, involving 60 million soldiers. Of those, an estimated 21 million were injured. Many of them lost limbs. To avoid placing an intolerable burden on the social welfare programs of the time, methods had to be devised to return the injured to military service or at least productive civilian life. These first PTs were called reconstruction aides or re-aides.

One of the first WWI re-aides, Col. Emma Vogel, went on to head the 1941 War Emergency Training Course, and later the Women's Medical Specialist Corps. The Special Women's Medical Service Corps Program for African Americans at Fort Huachuca, Arizona, was set up in 1943 and trained some of the first African American PTs.

Today, physical therapists serve in all branches of the U.S. military, as well as Veterans Affairs facilities.

WHAT THEY DON'T TELL YOU IN THE INTERVIEW

Every career has its not-so-pleasant moments. As in any medical career, PTs face the possibility of patients dying, particularly when they work with the elderly. Patients recovering from devastating accidents may be depressed. Patients with intellectual disabilities may become frustrated at being asked to do things they don't understand.

Some PTs love the energetic work environment, while others find it too physically demanding. After helping patients exercise all day, physical therapists may feel exercise fatigue themselves. Sometimes the challenge of finding a cause of pain can be too difficult. At times, a patient may not be able to tell the PT. This, too, takes a toll on physical therapists. Physical and mental burnout can and does occur.

The extensive education of physical therapists can prepare them well for the workplace. However, it can involve a lot of time and money. After graduation, PTs need to keep their licenses in good standing through continuing education units. These, too, can cost money and time.

Another difficult factor in a physical therapist's day can be paperwork. Today's health care system involves a lot of contact with health insurance agencies. Careful records of the treatment process need to be kept. Insurance companies have strict milestones by which they measure the need for physical therapy. They may refuse to cover further treatment, even if a patient's medical team thinks it's necessary. Most patients can't afford to pay for treatment themselves. These present very frustrating obstacles in a PT's life.

Today's health insurance system is as daunting to health care professionals as it is to patients.

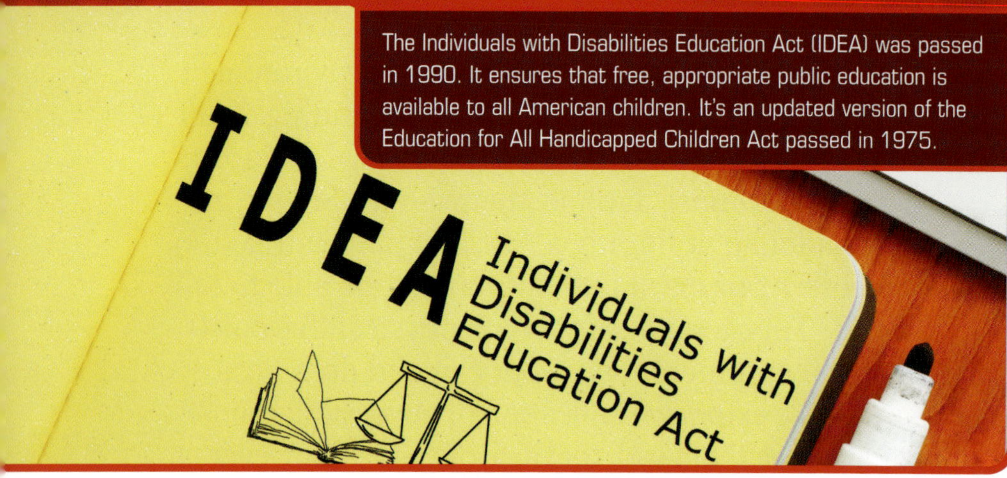

The Individuals with Disabilities Education Act (IDEA) was passed in 1990. It ensures that free, appropriate public education is available to all American children. It's an updated version of the Education for All Handicapped Children Act passed in 1975.

CHATTING WITH A PT

If you want to know what a profession is really like, you need to talk to someone who's in it. They will likely offer some advice and insight that can't be taught in school. Kelly C. is a physical therapist in Connecticut. In this section, she offers some views of her life as a school-based physical therapist, as well as her thoughts about the challenges and rewards of her career.

Where do you work?

I currently work in two school districts at several different schools for a total of eight schools per week. I have this type of arrangement because each district needed only a part-time PT. There isn't a huge need for PTs in schools. There is a greater need for occupational therapists (who help patients execute daily activities independently) and speech-language pathologists (who help patients with speech problems and/or difficulty swallowing). I have several schools because there are usually not enough children at a school to fill a day's worth of treatment. As you might imagine, scheduling can be tricky.

FINDING A MENTOR

In general terms, a mentor is a professional experienced in a field you're interested in who serves as a coach. They're usually older. A mentor can provide the sort of insights you can't find in textbooks. Their people skills and real-world experience are invaluable.

A PT mentor is an experienced professional who shepherds a newly graduated PT. Mentors can help with career, clinical, and professional issues. The APTA provides formal training for PT mentors.

What challenges do you face?

It's a great challenge to work around the student's class schedules. This is perhaps one of the hardest things about this type of setting. There is also not much space in a school to work. I don't have all the equipment available in a hospital or clinic, so I have to be creative and original.

The most difficult part of being a school-based PT is probably trying to decide what the child needs as a student, as opposed to what the child needs as a child. School-based therapy is meant to help the child benefit from their education. This means, for example, getting around the school, sitting for desk activities, and participating in physical education and recess. They may have difficulties that do not necessarily affect their education. As a professional trained to help reduce, prevent, and rehabilitate physical disabilities, I feel at times that I have to stop before I would like.

With whom do you work?

I work alongside teachers, but also other health care professionals, namely occupational therapists, speech-language pathologists, nurses, social workers, and psychologists. I occasionally speak with a doctor, but this is usually my request. This can be another challenge—making contact with a doctor despite both of our hectic schedules.

How did you decide to work in schools?

I used to work in an adult rehabilitation center with people who suffered strokes, head injuries, spinal cord injuries, and other medical issues. I found the amount of tasks—scheduling, paperwork, billing, ordering equipment, treatment, and meetings—made it difficult to get everything done in a day's work. This is what prompted me to leave that job and look toward the schools.

OCCUPATIONAL THERAPISTS

Occupational therapy is the profession most directly responsible for addressing problems with fine motor skills and coordination. Occupational therapists (OTs) and physical therapists often work closely together. The OT helps with activities of daily living (ADL), such as dressing (fastening buttons and zippers, and tying or velcroing shoes) and eating (manipulating a knife and fork). They also teach patients how to accomplish common household and workplace activities safely. They often focus on the use of hands and arms. OTs often work with people recovering from strokes. They also work with patients who have chronic conditions such as cerebral palsy or Alzheimer's.

In school settings, OTs may be asked to assist students with handwriting difficulties. More than PTs, OTs use psychology when working with their patients. Occupational therapists have a unique therapeutic approach to helping children manage their five senses within their environment.

OTs need to complete an accredited master's degree program in Occupational Therapy. Generally, these programs take two or three years. They also involve supervised clinical work. OTs need to be licensed. According to the BLS, OTs can expect to earn about $85,000 per year.

OTs will sometimes use toys to engage the interest of children or dementia patients.

What is the best part of being a PT?

The best part of being a PT is seeing someone improve their life because of the help that I've provided. This improvement may be allowing them to do something they couldn't before, providing a piece of equipment that makes life easier, or even offering information about how to get additional support.

PT is also a nice blend of medicine—everything from orthopedics, optometry, cardiopulmonary, pharmacology, etc. Someone who enjoys medicine and problem solving will find it to be a great profession. No two patients are alike, so it never gets boring.

How did you know you wanted to be a PT?

I knew I wanted to study physical therapy when I was applying to colleges. I had been an athlete through high school and had needed physical therapy myself. I was really interested in the posters they had on the walls of all the bones and muscles.

Do you have any suggestions for future PTs?

One strong suggestion I have for anyone thinking about being a PT is to spend time with a PT, preferably in a variety of settings. Prior to college, I was only aware of the sports medicine part of physical therapy—and only a small part of that. The physical therapy program was difficult for me because I didn't have any experience. Students should talk with practicing PTs, volunteer in clinics and hospitals, or set up days to shadow a PT. The education is difficult and requires many years. You don't want to find out it's not what you really wanted. The more experiences someone has, the better off they may be.

They may also encounter similar professions that appeal to them.

SO MANY CHOICES

As you can see, there are many choices available to someone considering a career as a PT. You can choose to work with children or the elderly, in a clinical setting, a school, or in patients' homes. You can be one of the first people to work with a patient post-op, or you can be the one who helps manages their chronic pain.

Another choice to consider is sports medicine. Many professional sports teams and dance companies have their own PTs. There are also dedicated sports medicine clinics. You can opt to become an APTA board certified specialist in sports medicine.

Did you know some cruise lines employ PTs? Cruise ships often have spa and wellness facilities that employ licensed PTs. Be sure to check the cruise line's website for any special certifications you might need.

Health and wellness retreats are big business. Luxury spas are another venue that employs PTs.

CHAPTER SIX

THE FUTURE OF PHYSICAL THERAPY

This is a good time to consider a career as a physical therapist. According to the U.S. Bureau of Labor Statistics, employment of physical therapists is expected to grow 17 percent in the next decade, much faster than most careers. Demand for physical therapy will grow with the increasing number of people needing it. Who are these people?

THE ELDERLY

People in the United States are living longer than ever before. Aging baby-boomers will be the fastest-growing age group in years to come. This group is more active than previous generations of elderly people. Many will suffer longer from conditions that make physical therapy necessary. Others will seek physical therapy to prevent future disabilities. Elderly people are more susceptible to strokes, heart attacks and age-related illnesses that require PT.

The growing elderly population also includes a large number of retiring physical therapists. This workforce will need to be replaced and in greater numbers to match the greater need for PTs specializing in geriatrics.

OBESITY AND DIABETES

Obesity is a serious problem that can lead to fatal diseases. According to the Centers for Disease Control and Prevention (CDC), between 2017 and 2020, the prevalence of obesity was 41.9 percent in the United States. Illnesses related to obesity cost about $173 billion each year. The rising rates of obesity and obesity-related illnesses increase the need for physical therapists. PTs combating obesity will focus on wellness programs. They will teach the importance of fitness and nutrition.

Obesity can lead to heart disease, stroke, and some types of cancer. One of the most common obesity-related illnesses is type 2 diabetes. PT help diabetic people to lower their blood sugar by exercise. They tailor a plan that the patient can accomplish safely. They may also help patients who've had surgical amputations due to the disease.

BABIES

Babies born early, or prematurely, need physical therapy as well. Forty weeks is the normal length for pregnancy. A child born before 37 weeks of pregnancy is considered premature. About 11 percent or 500,000 babies a year are born prematurely. This is a 30 percent increase in the last 25 years.

Although current medical technology can save many premature infants, they often face medical challenges. These can include physical disability, hearing loss, blindness, and chronic diseases like asthma. Initially, a PT will teach the parents how to safely hold their baby. Later they will evaluate

Some premature infants may require physical therapy for months or years to make sure they hit all their developmental milestones.

the baby's muscle tone and other factors. Early intervention by a PT will help these children live fuller and longer lives.

COVID-19

Physical therapists play an important role in treating COVID-19. Some patients benefit from PT to help them achieve a productive cough and clear their lungs. Patients who have spent a lot of time in bed benefit from PT to maintain muscle tone and joint mobility. They may also require help with walking and balance as they recover. There are also patients suffering from side effects such as "COVID toes" and the lingering symptoms of "long COVID."

UNIONS

A union is an organization of workers in a particular field or profession. Unions use a technique called collective bargaining. This means that instead of one person going to management with a concern, a union representing many employees—enough to disrupt business—present members' concerns.

Unions representing workers in many trades have negotiated better pay, uniform work hours, breaks, paid time off, and benefits for their members. A particular concern for unions representing health care workers is adequate staffing—that is, the number of patients each professional is responsible for. Having more time to tend to fewer patients isn't just good for the health care workers—it's better and safer for the patient.

There are several unions that represent health care workers, including:

- National Union of Health Care Workers (NUHW)
- United Food and Commercial Workers International Union (UFCW)
- Service Employees International Union (SEIU)
- International Federation of Professional and Technical Engineers (IFPTE)

BACK TO THE FUTURE

There are constant breakthroughs in medical technology and pharmacology. Physical therapists need to be aware of these changes and how they affect patient treatment. New treatments and medications allow people to live longer and healthier lives. They also make it possible to save people who would have died in the past.

However, cutting-edge medical technology is expensive, even with insurance. Pharmaceutical treatments are also expensive and can have side effects. For these reasons, many medical professionals recognize the value of programs like PT that preserve balance and ROM through carefully supervised exercise. Today many people are interested in holistic—or whole-body—medicine. These include practices such as yoga and acupuncture that have existed for centuries.

Yoga has been practiced for thousands of years as part of the Hindu religion. However, in Western culture, many people practice it solely as a form of exercise. Yoga postures are low-impact (no jumping or bouncing) and incorporate breathing exercises. Many people attend yoga programs as part of their overall wellness strategy. PTs who want to incorporate yoga into their clinical practice should seek professional certification as a yoga instructor/therapist.

Acupuncture is the practice of inserting needles into the skin at specific points to treat disorders. It's an ancient form of Chinese medicine. Acupuncture is an accepted and regulated part of physical therapy in Canada.

Practices such as acupuncture, yoga, and massage are considered complementary medicine. This means they're used in addition to Western medicine.

Being aware of the latest trends in wellness and complementary medicine is as important as keeping up with medical journals.

THINGS THAT CAN'T BE TAUGHT

Healing and caring are the two major components of a career in physical therapy. Healing is what you learn in school—how the human body works, how it responds to trauma, and ways to aid in recovery. You'll learn basic forms of therapy and how to execute them. You'll learn about medications and surgical techniques and complementary medicine. You might have a specialty in mind and focus on that until you've achieved board certification. Or you might start out in a general practice and decide on a specialty later—or not at all. You might find that helping all sorts of patients with different medical conditions is what fascinates you.

ERGONOMICS

Ergonomics, or human engineering, is the science of designing the things people use most often so that they can function safely and efficiently. This concept is often applied to business equipment and furnishings. In an office setting, people often sit for hours at a computer desk or perform the same movements over and over.

Ergonomic office chairs are designed to help people sit up straight and have proper support for their back. This helps prevent or relieve back pain. Ergonomic keyboards are designed to prevent carpal tunnel syndrome, a form of nerve damage that can affect people who type all day.

Other ergonomic devices include standing desks or height-adjustable desks that allow people to move around, instead of sitting in the same position all day. Cushioned rubber mats for people who stand at a workstation are another type of ergonomic device.

In the past, office workers often had neck pain from scrunching a phone between their shoulder and neck. Today, most people who use a phone for work use a headset and sit up straight in an ergonomic chair with proper lumbar support.

Caring is an aspect of the job that can't be taught or learned. It must be part of your personality—concern for other people and a desire to help them feel better. If you don't have it, you probably wouldn't be considering a career in health care, and you certainly won't succeed in a field like physical therapy.

PTs spend more time working directly with patients than other medical professionals. They need to have excellent people skills and an ability to think outside the box. In addition to the things you learn in school, there are situations that require thought and genuine caring such as:

- an elderly patient who doesn't get out much and wants to chat during their treatment
- learning about the form of folk medicine your patient has followed all their life and how it might affect their treatment
- finding a way to get an autistic or intellectually challenged person to follow your instructions
- explaining your treatment plan not just to a patient, but also their parent or caregiver

Physical therapy is a challenging and rewarding career with many exiting avenues to pursue. It's a great way to make a difference in your community and have a positive impact on your patients' lives. If it sounds like the right career for you, sit down with your parents and your guidance counselor and start planning.

If you're passionate about helping people feel better and live safer and more independent lives, PT might be the perfect career choice for you!

10 GREAT QUESTIONS TO ASK A PHYSICAL THERAPIST

Here are some questions you can ask a PT. If there are multiple practices nearby, try to visit a couple of different ones for different perspectives.

1. Are you a board-certified specialist?
2. Why did you choose that specialty?
3. Did you work as a PTA or aide before pursuing your degree?
4. Where did you go to school for your physical therapy degree?
5. Is this the only type of clinical setting you've worked in?
6. Why did you choose it?
7. If you could work in a different setting, what would it be?
8. Do you belong to any professional organizations?
9. Are there any books you recommend I read? Industry blogs or magazines that are worth following?
10. How has your job changed since the COVID-19 pandemic?

What other questions can you think of?

A career as a PT is a worthy goal for some who cares about helping people live happier healthier lives.

GLOSSARY

accreditation: An official recognition for having met a standard.

ailment: An illness or injury.

Alzheimer's disease: An illness that causes mental problems, such as extreme forgetfulness.

anatomy: The physical structure, especially internal, of a plant or animal.

arthritis: An illness that causes swelling of the joints, stiffness, and pain.

atrophy: Weakening or lessening in ability.

carpal tunnel syndrome: A condition of pain or weakness in a hand or wrist caused by repetitive movements.

cerebral palsy: A condition caused by brain damage at birth marked by a lack of muscle control.

chronic: Lasting a long time or occurring often.

coordination: Movement of body parts at the same time.

cystic fibrosis: A disease that results in thick mucus blocking air passages.

diabetes: A disorder that causes the body to produce an excessive amount of urine.

doctoral: Relating to the highest degree offered by a university.

evaluate: To examine something in order to judge its condition.

geriatric: Relating to the elderly.

inflammation: Swelling, redness, heat, and pain in an area of the body as a result of injury or infection.

ligament: Tissue in the body that connects bones at a joint or supports another body part.

massage: A treatment that involves rubbing or kneading the muscles.

mentor: A trusted guide or teacher.

motor skill: A function that involves precise movement of muscles with the intent to perform a specific act.

osteoporosis: A disease in which bones become brittle and break easily.

passive: Not actively participating.

physiology: A branch of biology that deals with how living things function.

polio: A severe infection that inflames the brain stem and spinal cord, sometimes leading to paralysis.

posture: The way a person carries his or her body.

rehabilitation: The process of making someone healthy again.

statistics: The branch of math that deals with interpreting data.

tendon: A cord of tissue that attaches a muscle to a bone or other body part.

FOR MORE INFORMATION

ACADEMY OF ORTHOPAEDIC PHYSICAL THERAPY

2920 East Ave. South
Suite 200
La Crosse, WI 54601
(800) 444-3982
Website: www.orthopt.org
Facebook: @OrthopaedicAPTA
Instagram: @apta_orthopaedic
AOPT is the APTA's academy dedicated to training orthopaedic specialists.

AMERICAN COLLEGE OF SPORTS MEDICINE

401 West Michigan Street
Indianapolis, IN 46202-3233
(317) 637-9200
Website: www.acsm.org
Facebook: @ACSMNews
Instagram: @acsm1954
The ACSM represents sports medicine professionals from 90 countries.

AMERICAN MEDICAL ASSOCIATION

AMA Plaza
330 N. Wabash Ave.
Suite 39300
Chicago, IL 60611-5885
(800) 262-3211
Website: www.ama-assn.org
Facebook: @AmericanMedicalAssociation
Instagram: @amermedicalassn

The AMA is a professional organization dedicated to the advancement of medicine in the U.S. They represent the medical profession in Washington, lobbying for legislation that affects the healthcare system.

AMERICAN PHYSICAL THERAPY ASSOCIATION

3030 Potomac Ave.
Suite 100
Alexandria, VA 22305-3085
(800) 999-2782
Website: apta.org
Facebook: @AmericanPhysicalTherapyAssociation
Instagram: @aptapics
The APTA is the preeminent professional organization for PTs, APTs, and others in the physical therapy field in the U.S.

CANADIAN PHYSIOTHERAPY ASSOCIATION

955 Green Valley Crescent
Suite 270
Ottawa, ON K2C 3V4
Canada
(800) 387-8679
Website: physiotherapy.ca
Facebook: @CPA.ACP
Instagram: @physiotherapycanada
The CPA is a national organization for physiotherapy professionals in Canada.

FEDERATION OF STATE BOARDS OF PHYSICAL THERAPY

124 West Street South
Third Floor
Alexandria, VA 22314

(703) 299-3100
Website: fsbpt.org
Facebook: @fsbpt
The FSBPT is the organization that administers the National Physical Therapy Exam.

NATIONAL ATHLETIC TRAINERS ASSOCIATION

1620 Valwood Parkway
Suite 115
Carrollton, TX 75006
(214) 637-6282
Website: www.nata.org
Facebook and Instagram: @nata1950
NATA represents the professional interests of certified athletic trainers.

NATIONAL CENTER FOR COMPLEMENTARY AND INTEGRATIVE HEALTH

National Institutes of Health
9000 Rockville Pike
Bethesda, MD 20892
(888) 644-6226
Website: nccih.nih.gov
Facebook: @nih.nccih
Instagram: @nih_nccih
The NCCIH conducts research on complementary medical products and practices.

NEW YORK PHYSICAL THERAPY ASSOCIATION

971 Albany-Shaker Road
Latham, NY 12110
(518) 459-4499
Website: nypta.org
Facebook: @NYPTAPage

The NYPTA is the New York branch of the APTA.

ONTARIO PHYSIOTHERAPY ASSOCIATION

110 Sheppard Avenue East
Suite 810
Toronto, ON M2N 6Y8
Canada
(800) 672-9668
Website: opa.on.ca
Facebook: @OntarioPT
Instagram: @ontariophysio
The OPA is the Ontario branch of the CPA.

AMERICAN ASSOCIATION OF SPORTS PHYSICAL THERAPY

1417 Shelby Street
Indianapolis, IN 46203
(317) 973-2163
Website: sportspt.org
Facebook: @AASPTAPTA
Instagram: @aaspta_apta
The AASPT is the branch of the APTA dedicated to sports medicine.

FOR FURTHER READING

Cartlidge, Cherese. *Skilled Jobs in Health Care*. San Diego, CA: ReferencePoint Press, Inc. 2021.

Endsley, Kezia. *Health and Fitness Professionals: A Practical Career Guide*. Lanham, MD: Rowman & Littlefield, 2019.

Given-Wilson, Rachel, and Therese Harasymiw. *Your Future as a Physical Therapist*. West Seneca, NY: Rosen Publishing, 2020.

Huddleston, Emma. *Work in the Health Care Industry*. San Diego, CA: BrightPoint Press, 2020.

Lanier, Wendy Hinote. *Become a Physical Therapy Assistant*. San Diego, CA: BrightPoint Press, 2023.

Mometrix Test Prep. *NPTE Secrets Study Guide - NPTE Exam Review for the National Physical Therapy Examination*. Beaumont, TX: Mometrix Media LLC, 2023.

Sambaumniel Publication. *Musculoskeletal Anatomy Coloring Book*. Independently published, 2020.

Wilcox, Christine. *Health Care Careers*. San Diego, CA: ReferencePoint Press, Inc. 2019.

INDEX

S

T

U

V

W

Y

ABOUT THE AUTHOR

KATHLEEN A. KLATTE is the author of many nonfiction books for children and teens. Topics range from animals and nature to constitutional law to unusual career choices. She lives in New York with one cat and far too many books and Legos.

PHOTO CREDITS

Photo Credits: Cover, p 1 wavebreakmedia/Shutterstock.com; pp. 1-96 Merydolla/Shutterstock.com; p. 5 ALPA PROD/Shutterstock.com; p. 6 Studio Romantic/Shutterstock.com; p. 7 Eray Adiguzel/Shutterstock.com; pp. 9, 14 Everett Collection/Shutterstock.com; p. 11 Hananeko_Studio/Shutterstock.com; p. 13 takasu/Shutterstock.com; p. 15 Atstock Productions/Shutterstock.com; p. 17 Microgen/Shutterstock.com; p. 18 Maksim Shmeljov/Shutterstock.com; p. 20 DC Studio/Shutterstock.com; pp. 21, 80 Monkey Business Images/Shutterstock.com; p. 23 NARONG JHANWATTANA/Shutterstock.com; p. 24 Dmytro Zinkevych/Shutterstock.com; p. 26 goodluz/Shutterstock.com; p. 29 Bill45/Shutterstock.com; pp. 29, 38 Prostock-studio/Shutterstock.com; p. 30 Microgen/Shutterstock.com; p. 34 Alex Kh/Shutterstock.com; p. 35 stockfour/Shutterstock.com; p. 36 Ground Picture/Shutterstock.com; p. 40 Branislav Nenin/Shutterstock.com; p. 42 Tyler Olson/Shutterstock.com; p. 44 Komsan Loonprom/Shutterstock.com; p. 46 Kostiantyn Voitenko/Shutterstock.com; p. 47 George Rudy/Shutterstock.com; p. 49 Zmaster/Shutterstock.com; p. 52 sasirin pamai/Shutterstock.com; p. 53 P Stock/Shutterstock.com; p. 55 AnnGaysorn/Shutterstock.com; p. 60 Sata Production/Shutterstock.com; p. 63 Gorodenkoff/Shutterstock.com; p. 65 Ground Picture/Shutterstock.com; p. 67 vinnstock/Shutterstock.com; p. 68 Jack_the_sparow/Shutterstock.com; p. 71 Daisy Daisy/Shutterstock.com; p. 73 Mikael Damkier/Shutterstock.com; p. 76 antoniodiaz/Shutterstock.com; p. 78 Ground Picture/Shutterstock.com; p. 81 Krakenimages.com/Shutterstock.com; p. 83 insta_photos/Shutterstock.com.